HAYNES E
RUGBᴙ

Owners' Workshop Manual

© Haynes Publishing • Written by **Boris Starling**

Published in July 2019

A catalogue record for this book is available from the British Library

ISBN 978 1 78521 662 6

Haynes Publishing, Sparkford, Yeovil,
Somerset BA22 7JJ, UK
Tel: +44 (0) 1963 440635
Website: www.haynes.com

Haynes North America, Inc.,
861 Lawrence Drive, Newbury Park,
California 91320, USA

Printed and bound in Malaysia

Cover image from Getty Images

Illustrations taken from the
Haynes VW Super Beetle
Owners Workshop Manual

Written by **Boris Starling**
Edited by **Louise McIntyre**
Designed by **Richard Parsons**

Safety first!

Like all sports, rugby has its hazards. Injuries can be caused by – well, pretty much everything, because that's rugby. There's a reason why former Samoan captain Peter Fatialofa gave his occupation as 'piano mover'. Rugby hurts. The best way to remain safe is not to play it. But if you insist: the best way to remain safe is to be a very fast, very scared winger who runs like stink the moment he gets the ball, and doesn't stop till he reaches the changing room.

Working facilities

A rugby pitch may be made of grass, sand, clay, snow (you what?) or artificial turf. It must be between 94 and 100 metres long and between 68 and 70 metres wide. The distance from the tryline to the 22-metre line must be – come on, you can work that out for yourself, you're surely not as dumb as you look. And from the halfway line to the 10-metre line? See, you're getting the hang of this already.

Contents

Introduction

As with many sports, rugby as we know it was invented by the English. As with other sports we invented, such as cricket, we like to keep the number of countries who play it down to a minimum so that we have a fighting chance of winning now and then. (We let this slip when it came to football, and look what happened. 53 years of hurt, and counting).

There's an old adage about football being a gentlemen's sport played by thugs and rugby being a thugs' sport played by gentlemen. Like all adages, it's only partly true, but the bit that is true speaks volumes for the appeal of the game. There's never any crowd trouble, despite the heroic quantities of booze consumed in the stands. The referee's word is law, and is accepted as such. And it's normal for opposing teams to spend an afternoon knocking seven bells out of each other and then the evening knocking seven pints back with each other: Canadian Norm Hadley and Englishman Jason Leonard began a lifelong friendship after Leonard belted Hadley as hard as he could at a lineout and Hadley asked 'is that the best you've got, princess?'

About this manual

The aim of this manual is to help you get the best value from rugby. It can do this in several ways. It can help you (a) decide what work must be done, and (b) tackle this work yourself, though you may choose to have much of it performed by external contractors such as the man who's the same shape as a refrigerator and seems to have cauliflower-shaped ears, the lanky beanpole with octopus arms, the yappy annoying bloke who you know without even needing to ask is a scrum-half, the flash git whose grooming routine would fill an entire issue of *GQ*, and the nervy guy built like a whippet and as keen to leave scorch marks.

The manual has drawings and descriptions to show the function and layout of the various components. Tasks are described in a logical order so that even a novice can do the work. Don't run before you can walk. Don't sidestep before you can run. Don't hand-off before you can sidestep. Don't sidestep before you can chip-and-chase. And don't showboat, ever, unless you want to be clattered hard by the opposition's most psychotic player and told 'we don't do that round here, sunshine.'

Dimensions, weights and capacities

Overall height

Of the tricky little pocket battleship with a low centre of gravity who wears 9... 5'6"
Of the centre with physical presence and a penchant for the crash ball .... 6'2"
Of the second row line-out jumper/enforcer .... 6'8"

Overall weight

Of an international back in 1979 .... 75kg (of which 5kg was sideburns)
Of an international back in 2019 .... 100kg (of which 0kg is sideburns)
Of an international forward in 1979.... 100kg (at 36% body fat)
Of an international forward in 2019.... 125kg (at 12% body fat)

Consumption

1979 .... Full English breakfast: Big Mac meal with extra fries for lunch; chicken tikka masala and pilau rice for dinner; 10 pints to drink.

2019... Porridge and fruit for breakfast; salmon, pasta and quinoa for lunch; chicken and vegetables for dinner; water and electrolytes to drink.

Engine

Stroke .... What you're going to give the guy in the row behind me if you don't clear it into touch NOW FOR THE LOVE OF GOD JUST KICK IT

Power... Several tons going through the front rows of international scrums as they pack down. Seriously. No place for the faint-hearted.

Bore .... The bloke you always find yourself next to at a match who has an encyclopaedic knowledge of the rules and isn't afraid to demonstrate this.

Redline .... Not when you've been punched, because you expect that.

Vehicle regulations

The aim of rugby is to score more points than the opposition, which is more or less the aim of most games (except Pointless). There are four ways to score points in rugby:

a) A try (5 points) when a team grounds the ball in the opposition's in-goal (the area between the tryline and the dead-ball line.)

b) A penalty (3 points) when a player kicks the ball from stationary between the goalposts and above the crossbar.

c) A drop goal (3 points) when a player drops the ball onto the ground and kicks it between the goalposts and above the crossbar.

d) A conversion (2 points), when after a try is scored a player kicks the ball from stationary between the goalposts and above the crossbar. Conversions are taken in line from where the try was scored.

The rules

The game usually lasts for 80 minutes, with players taking a break and

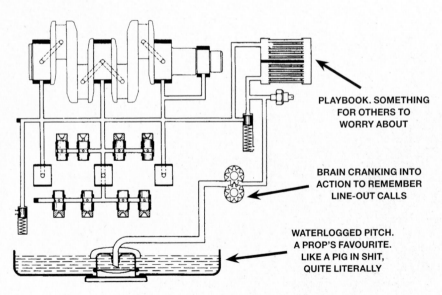

PLAYBOOK. SOMETHING FOR OTHERS TO WORRY ABOUT

BRAIN CRANKING INTO ACTION TO REMEMBER LINE-OUT CALLS

WATERLOGGED PITCH. A PROP'S FAVOURITE. LIKE A PIG IN SHIT, QUITE LITERALLY

FIG 13•1 **RUGBY: A FRONT ROW'S SCHEMATIC**

swapping ends after the first 40. It is played between teams of 15 on a grass field approximately 100m x 70m. These dimensions can vary according to Einstein's theory of relativity. For a professional player on a beautifully tended pitch, 100m is no distance at all. For a fat chain-smoking amateur prop on a pitch that resembles the second day of the Somme, 100m can be like Zeno's paradox, where the end never comes no matter how long you go for. (Don't mention either Einstein or Zeno to props, however. It just confuses them.)

The ball can be kicked in any direction. Sometimes, depending on the kicker's skill and the prevailing weather conditions, the ball may even go roughly where it was intended to. It can also be passed from hand, but only backwards. This particular proviso is the bit that always confuses Americans, who are used to quarterbacks hurling the ball straight down the field after yelling the kind of coded sequences usually reserved for the launch of nuclear weapons.

Come to think of it, lots of things about rugby confuse Americans, including:

a) the lack of helmets
b) the lack of ridiculous amounts of body padding
c) the capacity of the fans to down 10 pints in an 80-minute period without apparent ill effect

WHITEWASH, OF COURSE, NOT COCAINE. THIS IS NOT SOCCER

FIG 13·2 **MARKING OUT THE WHITE LINES**

d) and the distinct lack of players informing each other on a minute-by-minute basis that they are, in fact, the man.

Players can stop one another from running with the ball by tackling them. Tackles must be made with the arms – shoulder-charges and tripping are strictly prohibited – and must be below the neck. When the ball carrier is tackled, and the ball is on the ground and players from both sides contest the ball, a ruck is formed. When the ball carrier is tackled, the ball is held off the ground and players from both sides contest the ball, a maul is formed. Both rucks and mauls involve large, sweaty men grappling with each other in a manner rarely seen outside Turkish wrestling bouts.

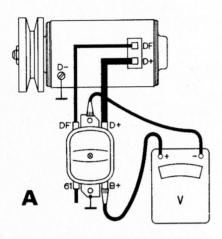

FIG 13•3 **POWER MEASUREMENTS FOR TWO 950KG PACKS AT POINT OF IMPACT**

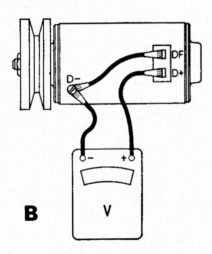

FIG 13•4 **TORTURE INSTRUMENT TO MAKE THE OPPOSITION HOOKER REVEAL THEIR LINEOUT CODES**

More rules...

When play is stopped for minor infringements, a scrum is used to restart the game. Scrums are basically more organised versions of rucks and mauls, and involve eight men on each side (the forwards) who bind together in three rows: three in the front and back rows, and two in the second row. Scrums are equal parts medieval skulduggery, applied Newtonian physics and those same large, sweaty men just wanting a hug but being too shy to ask for one directly.

When the ball goes off the pitch, play is restarted by a line-out, when the opposing forwards form two lines and jump for the ball as it's thrown in. In the olden days, when shirts were baggy and sideburns gargantuan, players were not allowed to lift each other, which meant that the line-out was more or less legalised mayhem: a couple of men jumping while the others punched each other. Now lifting is allowed, and teams work on routines so elaborate they should get an airing on Strictly.

As with quarterback play in American football, line-outs rely heavily on code words. For example, words beginning with 'P' might signal that the ball is going to the front of the line-out, while words beginning with 'S' mean the ball is going to the middle. Calling the word 'psychology' in this situation is a sure-fire way to confuse everybody.

The referee's a top bloke

Games are controlled by a referee, who, depending on the level of the match, may also have:

a) two assistant referees (touch judges, who take up position on either side of the pitch)
b) a fourth official to deal with substitutions
c) a TMO (television match official) to review important decisions
d) and 55,000 people in the stands who think they can do a better job than him, aren't shy of saying so, and suggest on a regular basis that the local branch of Specsavers could do with his custom.

Referees can show players a yellow card (sent off the pitch for 10 minutes) or a red card (sent off for the rest of the game). A referee may speak to any player, but only the captain of each team may speak to the referee without being asked. The referee's word is law, and is accepted as such: one of the best things about rugby is the way that a man half the size of everyone else on the pitch rules with a rod of iron.

The most famous referee in the world, and probably the best, is Nigel Owens of Wales. His one-liners, which have made him a cult figure, include:

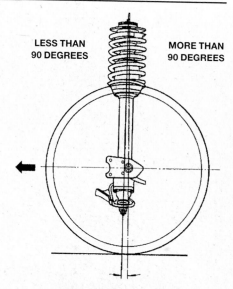

LESS THAN 90 DEGREES

MORE THAN 90 DEGREES

FIG 13•5 **THE REFEREE'S WHEEL TO MEASURE THE ANGLE OF THE SCRUM'S WHEEL**

a) 'You're both acting very immature' to Mike Brown and Yoann Huget during an England-France match
b) 'I don't think we've met before. I'm the referee. You do your job and I'll do mine' to a player who kept shouting for offences
c) 'This is not soccer' to anyone who feigns injury
d) 'Christopher!' to England captain Chris Robshaw, who was arguing with him. 'Sorry, sir,' Robshaw said before retreating.

Model range

Full Back (number 15)

The last line of defence. A good full back must be a secure tackler, a good kicker, an elusive runner and an expert catcher of high balls. A bad full back may as well carry a lollipop sign to wave through the opposition when they're anywhere near him. Full backs see the entire game unfolding in front of them and are therefore well positioned to point out their teammates' manifold shortcomings. Whether or not their teammates care to listen is another matter entirely.

Wings (14 and 11)

The speed demons who mainly operate near the touchlines. Like: sprinting for the line and diving extravagantly for tries. Dislike: tackling, getting their kit dirty. Many wings are small and lithe, though now and then a man-mountain who can also run fast is put out there, much to the dismay of the small, lithe man who now has to try and tackle him. Their proximity to the crowd means that the wings are subject to extensive advice and vociferous criticism, mainly from their own fans.

Centres (13 and 12)

Centres like to hunt in pairs and often make a point of being as different from each other as possible: one built like a brick outhouse who will never go round his opposite number when he can go through him instead, the other with dancing feet and deft hands. Now and then they get confused as to which is which and try to take on the other's mantle, with predictably hilarious results.

Fly-half (10)

The playmaker, who directs backline play and is usually the team's primary kicker. The fly-half is often a good footballer, which he will always remind you of, but not quite good enough to have made it as a professional, which he will never remind you of. The primary target of the opposition's back row, not only because tackling him is disruptive to his team's progress but also because it's so damn satisfying to mash his coiffure into the mud.

Scrum-half (9)

Small, yappy, annoying, never still. A cross between a Yorkshire terrier and Napoleon. The scrum-half is the link between forwards and backs, which allows him to bark orders at them all, which in turn allows them all to hate him equally. He's very equal opportunities like that. Usually the shortest and lightest player on the team, but often imagines himself as the tallest and heaviest, meaning he could start a fight in a phone box.

Props (1 and 3)

So called because they prop up the scrum. Usually 'big-boned', 'solid', 'stout', 'well-upholstered' or 'Falstaffian', props are as wide as they are tall, and constant abrasion to their heads in the scrum mean their ears can resemble small cauliflowers. Props care little about the result of the match but greatly about their opposite number, being equally keen to best him on the pitch and get hog-whimperingly drunk with him in the bar afterwards.

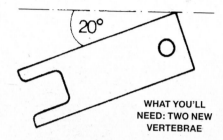

WHAT YOU'LL NEED: TWO NEW VERTEBRAE

FIG 13·6 **OPTIMUM ANGLE OF TIGHT-HEAD BORING IN ON THE OPPOSITION HOOKER**

Hooker (2)

So called because he hooks the ball back through the scrum. The hooker packs down between the props and likes to think of himself as more intelligent than both of them. He is also responsible for throwing the ball in at the line-out. The uncharitable would say that the hooker is too small to be a prop, too slow to be a back and too short-tempered to be anything other than a hooker. The uncharitable would not be too far off the mark.

Locks (4 and 5)

The tallest men in the team, whose job is to jump in the line-outs, use their long arms to grapple in mauls Mr Tickle style, and also act as on-the-pitch enforcers (a role to which they apply themselves with considerable gusto). Are obliged to bind in the scrum by putting their hand between the prop's legs and grip the waistband of his shorts, which is the kind of operation usually only carried out by trained farmyard vets.

Flankers (6 and 7)

The quickest members of the pack, who bind onto the side of the scrum so that they can detach quickly. Usually divide themselves by blindside (6) and openside (7), referring to which side of the scrum they select and how much of the pitch they have to cover. Blindside tends to be larger and tackles like a threshing machine; openside smaller and quicker, often letting the backs do all the fancy stuff before taking a pass two metres from the line and scoring a try.

Number 8 (er, 8)

A position so unimaginative they couldn't even think of a name for it – which is ironic, since the number 8 is often one of the best athletes in the team. Number 8s think they can jump like locks and run like centres. Some even think they can kick like fly-halves, a delusion greeted by their teammates adopting the pose of Munch's 'The Scream' every time the Number 8 looks like putting boot to ball.

Vehicle equipment

Jersey

Back in the day, the rugby jersey was just that: large, thick, made of cotton, and weighing 2.5 tonnes by the end of a rainy match. Man-made fibres began to make their appearance come professionalism in the mid-1990s (that is, a good 15–20 years after football: let no one accuse amateur rugby of lagging behind the times), and in the early 2000s jerseys became increasingly close-fitting.

This was largely welcomed by backs, who saw themselves as lithe and chiselled. Less so by the front row, for whom this new fashion simply accentuated the convex, stag-night-at-the-darts nature of their physiques.

Shorts

Used to be very long, in the manner of Victorian bathing suits. Then became very short indeed. Short as in hotpants short, though no fashion designer who ever put out a pair of hotpants ever envisaged a rugby player's legs emerging from them. Now stabilised somewhere between the two extremes.

Socks

More resistant to change than the two above, though not totally. Often rolled down even at international level with the kind of scruffiness that used to give school PE teachers conniptions.

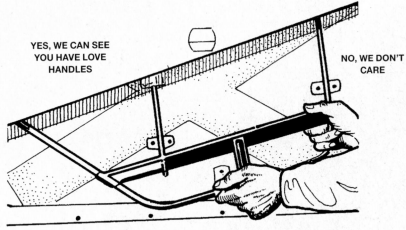

YES, WE CAN SEE YOU HAVE LOVE HANDLES

NO, WE DON'T CARE

FIG 13•7 **LASER FITTING THE RUGBY JERSEY**

Boots

Like the Ford Model T, used to come in any colour as long as they were black. Forwards' boots were built up around the ankle and could have doubled as WWI military issue. Nowadays, are available in all colours and have become increasingly lightweight, which is all well and good until a 20-stone man stands on your foot and you find that your hi-tech lightweight boot protects your metatarsal about as well as a bedroom slipper does.

Mouthguard

Obligatory and sensible, if you don't want your teeth to be spread across the length and breadth of the pitch (no more than 100m and 70m respectively, as you'll know if you were paying attention in section 1.) Makes talking quite hard, but then again you don't play rugby for the conversation.

Scrumcap

Worn not to prevent concussion (it doesn't) but abrasion. Certain players can be spotted from a long way off by their choice of scrumcap. As with wearing brightly coloured boots, this puts the pressure on the wearer to play well, as it's noticeable when they don't.

Scrum machine

Basically, a giant garden roller with pads attached against which forwards can practise scrummaging.

Ball

A rugby ball is a prolate spheroid essentially elliptical in profile. Yes, I am fun at parties. As with the jersey, old school models, which retained water and weight, have been replaced by synthetic waterproof versions, often with small knurls in the surface to aid grip. Just as football hipsters hanker after the black and white Adidas Telstar balls of the 1970s, so do rugby hipsters reserve a special place in their hearts for the Adidas Wallaby of the same era – light brown with black ends.

Kicking tee

A small plastic mount for place kicks. Before tees came in, a kicker would have to make a mound of mud for the ball. Some took this more seriously than others, and none more so than former England full back Bob Hiller. His meticulous approach once prompted a spectator to shout, 'Oi! Hiller! You want a shovel?' to which Hiller, in cut-glass tones, replied, 'Why don't you lend me your mouth? That's big enough.'

European models

International rugby in Europe revolves around the Six Nations tournament, held every February and March. Six nations – who'd have thunk it? – compete every year over five weekends, with each team playing every other team once, and home ground advantage alternating from one year to the next. Four points are awarded for a win, two for a draw and none for a loss. One bonus point is awarded for scoring four or more tries in a match, and one also for losing by seven points or fewer.

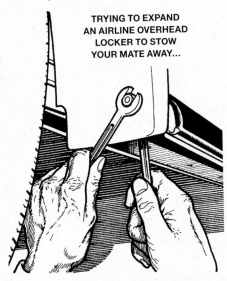

TRYING TO EXPAND
AN AIRLINE OVERHEAD
LOCKER TO STOW
YOUR MATE AWAY...

FIG 13•8 .... BECAUSE, YOU KNOW, RUGBY
HIGH JINKS AND ALL THAT

The six nations that compete in the tournament are:

1. England
Every other team in the Six Nations always seems to want to beat England even more than anyone else. With Wales, Scotland and Ireland, this stems from historical antipathy and size disparity. For France, it's mainly because they're French and, you know, Agincourt, Waterloo etc etc. With Italy, it's because they've played England 25 times in their history and never won.

2. France
French rugby is schizophrenic in two ways. First, the division between forwards and backs is more pronounced than usual, with the forwards tending to be gnarly hard men from the Basque Country and the backs handsome dilettantes from Paris. Second, the disparity between the team's play from one week to the next. At their best, France are the most glorious sight not just in world rugby but maybe all sport. At their worst, they're unwatchably terrible.

3. Ireland
Comprises both Northern Ireland and the Republic, which is just the way it's been for a long time rather than some

grand political statement. As with all the teams, their fortunes vary, but one thing remains constant: Dublin is the most popular destination for visiting fans, and it's no accident that Guinness sponsors the Six Nations.

4. Italy

There are question marks about their participation, now they've lost 22 matches in a row, but now and then they spring a surprise, such as famously flummoxing the England team in 2017 with a radical but entirely legal interpretation of the ruck laws (when England asked referee Romain Poite how they were supposed to deal with this, Poite replied with magnificent Gallic insouciance 'I am a referee, not a coach.')

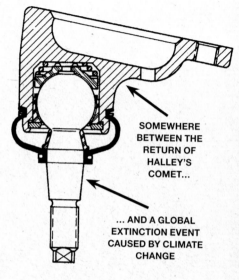

SOMEWHERE BETWEEN THE RETURN OF HALLEY'S COMET...

... AND A GLOBAL EXTINCTION EVENT CAUSED BY CLIMATE CHANGE

FIG 13•9 **CALCULATING THE EXACT DATE OF ITALY'S NEXT SIX NATIONS WIN**

5. Scotland

Use the thistle as their symbol, ever since the pained yelp of a Viking invader who'd stepped barefoot on one alerted the Scottish defenders. In 1990, with Scotland fuming at Margaret Thatcher's decision to apply the poll tax to them first, the Scottish side beat England to win the Grand Slam. England captain Will Carling was so unpopular north of the border that an Edinburgh pub put his face in the trough of a urinal, alongside those of Thatcher and Saddam Hussein – and Carling was apparently a more frequent target than the other two put together.

6. Wales

Their club game is often a mess, but their national team punches above its weight. The 1977 side was inspired by their captain Phil Bennett's speech before the match against England. 'Look what these bastards have done to Wales. They've taken our coal, our water, our steel. They buy our homes and live in them for a fortnight every year. What have they given us? Absolutely nothing. We've been exploited, raped, controlled and punished by the English. They've even knocked my Auntie Gladys' house down. That's who you're playing this afternoon.'

Rest of the world models

International rugby in the southern hemisphere revolves around the Championship, which comprises four nations:

New Zealand (The All Blacks)

The most famous and successful team in rugby history: the only team to have won the World Cup three times, and the only team to have a winning record against every other nation. Also known for the haka, the Maori war dance that precedes each of their matches. The fearsome and slickly choreographed modern haka is in stark contrast to the ones performed in the 70s, which look like a rather inept troupe of Morris dancers. Opposing teams have tried various methods of confronting the haka –

Wales refused to move when it was ended, Ireland marched right into it, the French advanced in an arrowhead – but perhaps the most memorable response was from Tonga, who performed their own dance, the Sipi Tau, during the haka. Before losing heavily.

Australia (The Wallabies)

Going through a bit of a slump at the moment, but usually consistently amongst the world's best (twice world champions and twice runners-up), which is pretty impressive given that rugby is at best the country's fourth most popular sport, behind cricket, AFL (Aussie Rules) and rugby league. Ahyeahlookmate no worries put another shrimp on the barbie.

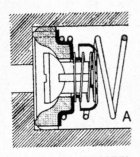 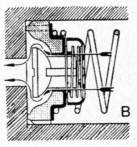 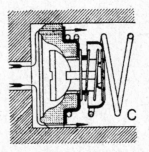

PUT YOUR LEFT FOOT IN   **TAKE YOUR LEFT FOOT OUT**   **SHAKE IT ALL ABOUT**

FIG 13•10 **PERFORMING THE HAKA: A BEGINNER'S GUIDE**

South Africa (The Springboks)

Once a symbol of white apartheid, now much more multiracial. Pride themselves on their physicality: a traditional Springbok forward likes nothing more than a good hard 'skrum'. Former Number 8 Tiaan Strauss reputedly used to practise his tackling by riding a quad bike up alongside wildebeest on his family farm, leaping off the bike onto the nearest wildebeest and seeing how long it took him to bring the animal to a halt. The Springbok fans heartily approved: the RSPCA probably less so.

Argentina (The Pumas)

A great place to tour, especially if you like Malbec and steaks. Often very much in the French mould of matinee idol backs and hard-as-nails forwards such as Federico Mendez, who aged 18 laid out England's giant lock Paul Ackford with a single punch. Ackford was at the time a Detective Inspector, leading his second row partner, Sergeant Wade Dooley, to opine 'you can tell which copper works behind a desk, can't you?'

Other nations

The Pacific islands of Fiji, Samoa and Tonga are all hotbeds of rugby but tend to lose most of their best players to the higher-ranked rugby nations (and, particularly in Samoa's case, American Football too). Given the strength, speed and natural ability of the Pacific Islanders, if they could ever get to keep all their players then the rest of the world might as well not bother turning up.

Two nations which do have the money to lift their teams into the top flight over the next few years are Japan and the USA. Japan beat South Africa in the 2015 World Cup, perhaps the greatest shock in rugby history. The USA are reigning Olympic rugby champions, though mainly because 15-a-side rugby last featured in the Olympics in 1924. But it still counts, right?

After Japan beat South Africa in the 2015 World Cup, fans shared a train back from Brighton to Victoria. At Victoria, the South African fans got off first and formed a guard of honour for the Japanese fans to walk through in appreciation of their team's victory.

Global marketplace

The Rugby World Cup takes place every four years. The current format comprises 20 teams, grouped into four groups of five. The winner and runner-up of each group go through to the quarter-finals, after which each match is a straight knockout.

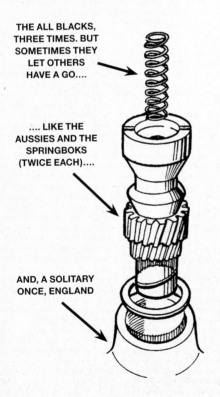

THE ALL BLACKS, THREE TIMES. BUT SOMETIMES THEY LET OTHERS HAVE A GO....

.... LIKE THE AUSSIES AND THE SPRINGBOKS (TWICE EACH)....

AND, A SOLITARY ONCE, ENGLAND

FIG 13•11 **THE WILLIAM WEBB ELLIS CUP**

1987

The inaugural tournament, held in New Zealand. Rugby is still an amateur game, and it shows: one journalist writes of England's Mickey Skinner being 'under the impression, not altogether inaccurate, that he is attending an end-of-season piss-up.' In the opening match, New Zealand's John Kirwan beats half the Italian side to score a try. Years later, Kirwan will coach Italy, marry an Italian and claim Italian citizenship, telling the story of how he drives to the government office to get his Italian passport like a New Zealander, careful and measured, but drives back, new passport in top pocket, like an Italian: one hand out of the window, the other hand on the horn, and going for every gap in the traffic whether it exists or not. New Zealand beat France in the final.

1991

England, Ireland and France co-host. Wales lose to Western Samoa, and express relief that at least they weren't playing the whole of Samoa. England and France play a quarter-final in Paris, which is as close to war as sport gets: David Kirk, who captained the 1987 New Zealand side, says on the commentary: 'Jeez, these guys really hate each other.'

1995

South Africa host and win the tournament for the first time since their apartheid-era sporting ban was lifted. The tournament sees the rise of rugby's first global superstar, the giant Jonah Lomu, who rides roughshod over every team he plays. New Zealand beat Japan 145-17, and no one likes a bully. South Africa beat New Zealand in the final amid accusations that the All Blacks were deliberately poisoned ('Suzie the waitress' being the chief suspect, rather like the 'man on the grassy knoll' at the JFK assassination). Clint Eastwood makes Invictus, a movie of the Springboks' victory. When Nelson Mandela dies in 2013, people tweet condolences over pictures of Morgan Freeman.

1999

England, Scotland, Ireland, Wales and France hold matches. The first four don't do very well: Wales play the whole of Samoa this time and lose again. The fifth, France, look to be heading out in the semi-final, 24-10 down against New Zealand, when out of nowhere they start to play rugby of the gods, putting 33 points on the All Blacks and winning 43-31. When asked to account for the turnaround, their captain Raphael Ibanez shrugs expansively. 'The only explanation,' he says, 'is that we are French.'

THIS IS A RAZOR. MOST PROPS HAVE NO IDEA WHAT IT IS

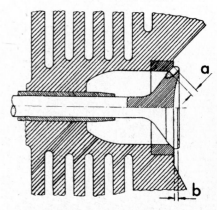

FIG 13•12 **THINGS THAT MAY BE A MYSTERY TO SOME RUGBY PLAYERS, #7487**

2003

Australia hold the tournament, and show themselves gracious and generous hosts by beating Namibia 142-0. They upset New Zealand in the semi-final, a match marked by their scrum-half George Gregan telling the All Blacks 'four more years, boys, four more years' as the game ticks away.

England beat Australia in the final with a Jonny Wilkinson drop goal at the end of extra time. His mum misses the whole thing as she's shopping in her local supermarket. England return home to a packed Heathrow and a million people on the streets of London for a parade a few weeks later. Not that the English public are desperate for sporting success or anything.

2007

France host, and lose in the semi-final to England: a scarcely credible result given that England lost a pool match 36-0, are rumoured to have mutinied against their coach, and somehow start to snatch victory from the jaws of defeat. For England fans used to their teams being amiably hopeless (2003 notwithstanding), this is rather discombobulating. France themselves only reach the semi after referee Wayne Barnes misses a forward pass in the build-up to their decisive try

against New Zealand. All Black fans refuse to complain and tell Barnes he's welcome in their country anytime. Air traffic control at Charles de Gaulle reports incidents of porcine aviation. South Africa beat England in the final.

2011

New Zealand host the tournament for the first time in 24 years, and win it for the first time in 24 years. England are pretty average on the pitch, and make more headlines off it by becoming involved in a scandal involving dwarf-tossing in a Queenstown bar. Wales reach the semi-final and lose to France in a contentious match. New Zealand just about hang on to beat France in the final, thus throwing off their 'chokers' tag.

2015

New Zealand become the first team to win back-to-back tournaments. England become the first hosts to be eliminated in the pool stage after losing to Wales (closely) and Australia (not closely). New Zealand and Australia play the final at Twickenham, thus depriving south-west London of 84% of its bar staff for the duration of the match. A small boy runs onto the pitch after the match and gets closer to the All Blacks than most of their opponents have. New Zealand centre Sonny Bill Williams gives the boy his winner's medal.

**SCALE: 1 IN
1,000,000,000,000**

FIG 13•13 **RESERVOIR FOR ALL THE BEER DRUNK DURING A WORLD CUP**

⚠ Touring cars

Touring is a staple of the rugby experience – 'what goes on tour stays on tour' – and the most famous touring side of them all is the British and Irish Lions. The schedule has varied over the years, but currently they tour every four years to South Africa, Australia and New Zealand in turn (thus visiting each of those countries only every 12 years) and they comprise the best players from England, Scotland, Ireland and Wales.

Lions folklore is replete with events on – and, more usually, off – the pitch.

1974

The tourists to South Africa enter into the spirit of things with particularly egregious vigour. On the pitch, determined to get their retaliation in first, the Lions come up with the '99' call – for every player to hit whichever member of the opposition is nearest them, on the grounds that the referee won't send all of them off. The '99' call is mainly the preserve of the forwards, but full back JPR Williams sprints enthusiastically across the pitch to lamp a Springbok whenever he is asked.

1977

Moss Keane, a last-minute call-up with a pathological fear of flying, is in such a state that he has a crash en route to the airport. He leaves his mother a message: 'The car's at the airport, it's written off, see you in four months.'

'Wanda from Wanganui', doing her bit for Kiwi patriotism, tells the press that she's slept with four of the Lions, describing them as 'lousy lovers, boring, self-centred, ruthless, always on the make and anything but exciting bedmates. Give me the down-to-earth Kiwi male any day.'

1980

Lions centre Ray Gravell tackles the Orange Free State fly-half after the ball has gone. The ref penalises and castigates him for the late tackle. 'Sorry, ref,' Gravell replies. 'I got there as quickly as I could.'

1997

Living With Lions, the first behind-the-scenes documentary of a Lions tour, comes out. It features Jim Telfer's 'this is your Everest' speech. Every person who watches it would put their boots on and go out and play for the Lions there and then.

Since then, professionalism has meant that most of these stories are things of the past (or at least are kept firmly under wraps by the professional social media team).

Vehicle league tables

The Gallagher Premiership

England's 12 best club teams, with the bottom club relegated each year and replaced by the winner of the Championship, the second tier league. Stalwarts of the Premiership include:

a) Bath, whose Recreation Ground (always just 'the Rec') is one of the most beautiful stadia in rugby anywhere in the world, and who along with Leicester ruled the roost in the days of amateur rugby.

b) Gloucester, whose infamous Shed stand is equal parts a Coliseum crowd of ancient Romans come to watch the annual Christians vs Lions derby, a mosh pit at a heavy metal concert and a gigantic stag night. The chants of 'Glaaaaaarster' can make one word stretch for most of a half of rugby.

c) Harlequins, London fancy dans whose multi-coloured jesters' shirts give a clue as to how they like to be seen.

d) Saracens, who've been champions more often than not in recent years, and whose all-star line-up will probably ensure that doesn't change too much in the foreseeable future.

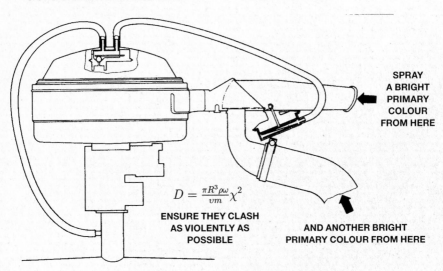

SPRAY A BRIGHT PRIMARY COLOUR FROM HERE

$$D = \frac{\pi R^3 \rho \omega}{vm}\chi^2$$

ENSURE THEY CLASH AS VIOLENTLY AS POSSIBLE

AND ANOTHER BRIGHT PRIMARY COLOUR FROM HERE

FIG 13•14 **MAKING RUGBY JERSEYS: A SIMPLE GUIDE**

The Pro 14

Like the Premiership, but with 14 teams rather than 12 (you can rarely accuse rugby of not doing what it says on the tin) and involving sides from – deep breath – Ireland, Italy, Scotland, South Africa and Wales. Yes, South Africa, even though it's thousands of miles away and even though other South African club sides play in Super Rugby (see below). Then again, this is a world in which Australia can compete in the Eurovision Song Contest.

The Top 14

Like the Pro 14, but exclusively French. The word 'top' must be said in a quick, mildly high-pitched voice, as though on cult French TV series Eurotrash, for maximum effect. In the amateur days, when Racing 92 club was called simply Racing Club, its players – can you tell they're French? – sometimes used to

IF WE GIVE IT ONE MORE TWIST, WE CAN GET ANOTHER COUPLE OF TEAMS IN....

FIG 13•15 **TINKERING WITH THE FORMAT**

play in berets, wearing pink bow ties, in long white trousers or dressed as pelote players (not all at the same time, obviously). Some of them even went on to found a boutique. You can imagine English props of a certain era founding a boutique, but not in this world or any conceivable parallel one.

The winner of the Premiership might not be the winner of the Premiership. When the league finishes, the second and third teams have a play-off, and the leading team plays the winner of this to decide who's champion.

Super rugby

15 teams from New Zealand, Australia, South Africa and Japan. Dominated, unsurprisingly, by teams from New Zealand, who win on average two in every three championships. In general, Super Rugby teams have much better names than their European counterparts, such as Sunwolves.

Weekend driving

The professional game might be rugby's showpiece and shop window, but the amateur game played up and down the country every weekend is still the game's grass roots. Pitches with 45 degree slopes, changing rooms whose showers last had hot water sometime around the Suez crisis, goalposts which make the Leaning Tower of Pisa look like the epitome of perpendicularity (is that even a word?) – these are the lynchpins of the amateur game.

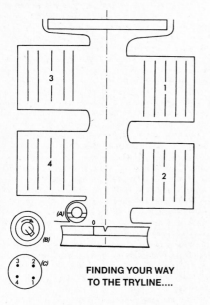

FIG 13•16 **... WHEN YOUR BRAIN'S STILL QUICK ENOUGH TO SEE THE GAP, BUT YOUR FEET ARE TOO SLOW TO MAKE IT**

FINDING YOUR WAY TO THE TRYLINE....

The brilliant ringer
Someone's mate's mate who turns up one day. Doesn't look up to much, but the moment you see him with ball in hand, you know he's good. He always picks the right lines to run, and – uniquely at this level – can catch a ball and pass it on without needing to bring it into his chest first.

The ancient prop
In his fifties, perhaps even older. Moves so slowly around the pitch as to risk warping the space-time continuum. But when it comes to front-row play and its dark arts, he has forgotten more than Severus Snape would ever have known, and loves nothing more than handing out an object lesson in said dark arts.

The metrosexual
Oh, there's always one. Waxes his chest, fake tan, gym-honed muscles, brings hair products for the shower. Can just about get away with it if he's good. All bets are off if he's not.

All the gear and no idea
Compression shorts? Check. Compression socks below regular socks? Check. Body protector? Check. Shoulder pads? Check. For the love of God, mate. It's Newton Abbot 3rds vs Burton Bradstock 4ths.

The shouter

Always yelling at his teammates. And never encouragingly, either. Everything good that happens is down to him; everything bad that happens is down to someone else. All his teammates are secretly praying that one of the opposition will fill him in when the ref's not looking.

The psycho

The smaller they come, the more psycho they are. A rugby version of Begbie from Trainspotting. They hide it well most of the time, but all they need is a trigger – and that can be something most people wouldn't even notice – and their eyes glaze over, and you know you're in a whole world of pain.

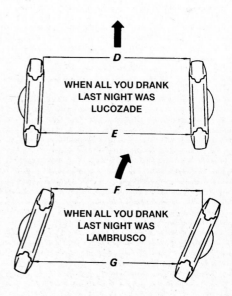

WHEN ALL YOU DRANK
LAST NIGHT WAS
LUCOZADE

WHEN ALL YOU DRANK
LAST NIGHT WAS
LAMBRUSCO

FIG 13·17 **PARALLAX VIEWS
OF A RUGBY PITCH**

The paceman

Winger who keeps himself in shape and is pretty quick – which is to say, by everyone else's standards is Usain Bolt. Can't tackle. Can't pass. Can hardly catch, and ideally needs the ball presented to him on a plate as though by a silver-service butler.

The newbie

Doesn't understand the rules. Is put on the subs' bench for the first half in the hope that he'll pick it up as he goes along, but instead he ends up thinking that he's already playing, and leathers the nearest member of the opposition when they come sprinting past him.

The hungover

Turns up reeking like a brewery. His eyes are pinholes in his face, he's bought the nearest garage's entire stock of sports drinks, and his hair looks as though he's just taken his scrumcap off without undoing the straps first. He may need to take a moment five minutes into the match to deposit the contents of his stomach at the base of the goalpost.

The prodigy

Half everyone else's age and twice as good. Would get a good kicking for this impudence from the old guard, but they can't get near enough to him to administer it.

Famous models

Rugby fans love nothing more than picking their all-time XV, arguing about their selection, criticising everyone else's selection, and so on. This is not so much an attempt at one of those as a XV taken from the modern era – that is, beginning with the 1987 World Cup.

15. Serge Blanco (France)

Chain-smoking genius. 'If Blanco ran in the snow,' his teammate Franck Mesnel once said, 'he would leave no footprints.' Once, when an opposition player complained that one of the French team had bit him, Blanco took one look at the evidence and said: 'These are not the marks of the French teeth,' thus proving himself an expert in orthodontics as well as a sublime rugby player.

WARNING

The fact that rugby fans like to argue about this kind of stuff, and the fact that rugby fans like a jar or five, means there is more than adequate potential for this to go all Paul Calf: 'I like drinking, like a laugh, chat, you know – bit of a debate, argument, scrap, fight, punch-up, break some bloke's nose. I like life.'

14. David Campese (Australia)

Purveyor of the finest goose-step seen on a rugby pitch, and a dab hand at the no-look over-the-shoulder pass too. Never afraid of voicing an opinion, 99% of the time aimed at the English. Remembered fondly by Lions fans for giving away the try that won the 1989 series. They may have reminded him of it a few times over the years.

13. Brian O'Driscoll (Ireland)

Known as BOD, more for the 'God' connotations than any similarity with 1970s animated children's TV series 'Bod'. The only player in the modern era to have gone on four Lions tours. Scored a sensational try in his first Lions test against Australia in 2001: dislocated his shoulder in the first minute of the first 2005 Test against the All Blacks when he was captain.

12. Tim Horan (Australia)

One of the most complete players ever: solid in defence, tactically astute, great eye for a gap and full of gas (especially, and quite literally, in the 1999 World Cup semi-final when he played despite having not eaten for two days owing to a bout of gastroenteritis). Known as 'Helmet' for his hairstyle, which remained rock solid even in the most brutal of Test matches.

11. Jonah Lomu (New Zealand)

A man apart, in every way. 'Rugby is a team game,' read one message to the New Zealand team hotel before the 1995 World Cup semi-final against England. 'All 14 of you, give it to Jonah.' After the match, in which Lomu scored four tries, England captain Will Carling said: 'There are 14 All Blacks in the shower right now, and Jonah's in the car wash down the road.' Died in 2015 of a heart attack related to a long-standing kidney condition.

10. Jonny Wilkinson (England)

Won England the 2003 World Cup at the death, and looked like he hated every minute of the adulation that ensued, which of course endeared him to people even more. A total obsessive when it came to training. Kicked like a metronome, tackled like a truck. His injury list is like something out of the Spanish Inquisition.

9. Joost van der Westhuizen (South Africa)

Heartbeat of the side that won the 1995 World Cup. Played the final with two broken ribs, and still managed to do what England hadn't and tackle Lomu. Scored 38 tries in 89 Tests, which is a return a winger would have been proud of. In retirement suffered sex scandals before being diagnosed with motor neurone disease, from which he died in 2017.

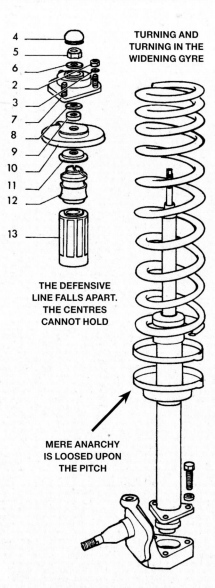

TURNING AND TURNING IN THE WIDENING GYRE

THE DEFENSIVE LINE FALLS APART. THE CENTRES CANNOT HOLD

MERE ANARCHY IS LOOSED UPON THE PITCH

FIG 13·18 **WHAT HAPPENS WHEN DAVID CAMPESE RUNS AT YOU**

1. Jason Leonard (England)

Barking carpenter (that is, 'he is from the Essex town of Barking', not 'he is insane') known as the Fun Bus. His mother refused to come and watch him play as she 'didn't want to see my little boy get hurt.' (Her little boy weighed 18 stone and had a neck the width of the Channel Tunnel.) Played in two World Cup Finals 12 years apart and straddled the amateur and professional eras.

2. Sean Fitzpatrick (New Zealand)

Iconic All Blacks hooker who was part of the team that won the first ever World Cup. Not shy of pointing out to the referee any offences he may have missed. Famous for a contretemps with Australian hooker Phil Kearns, which ended with Kearns making a hand gesture to confirm that yes, he would be attending Fitzy's barbecue and yes, he would like two sausages.

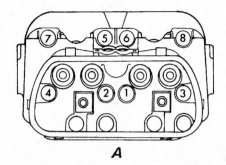

A

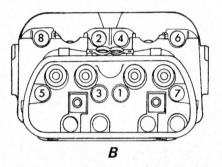

B

FIG 13•19 **SOME OF THE EARLY SCRUM FORMATION IDEAS. YOU CAN SEE WHY THEY NEVER CAUGHT ON**

The subs' bench

16: Keith Wood (Ireland)
17: Tendai Mtawarira (South Africa)
18: Adam Jones (Wales)
19: Victor Matfield (South Africa)
20: Sam Warburton (Wales)
21: George Gregan (Australia)
22: Dan Carter (New Zealand)
23: Bryan Habana (South Africa)

3. Os du Randt (South Africa)

'Os' as in 'Ox'. Like Leonard, played in two World Cup Finals 12 years apart: unlike Leonard, won them both. Lions fans remember him being knocked over by Scott Gibbs in the second 1997 Test, even though Os was a prop and Gibbs a centre (then again, Gibbs was known as 'the world's fastest prop' thanks to his physique and attitude).

4. Martin Johnson (England)

Monobrowed supreme leader of the England World Cup winning team. Never a man to use five words where one would do, or indeed any words where none would do. Was informed before the 2003 match against Ireland that England were lining up for the anthems on Ireland's 'lucky side'. Informed the official in question where he could shove this information.

5. John Eales (Australia)

Nicknamed 'Nobody' as in 'nobody's perfect'. Could do everything. A natural athlete who could jump, run, tackle and even kick well enough to be Australia's front-line kicker for a while, playing in a position where putting boot to ball is about as rare as a Scotsman buying a round. Looked too nice and gentle to play in the thick of things. Clearly was anything but.

6. Michael Jones (New Zealand)

At his peak, maybe the perfect rugby player. Refused to play on Sundays due to his strict religious beliefs, leading to one fan pointing out before a World Cup semi-final in England that by the time the match kicked off it would actually be Monday in New Zealand.

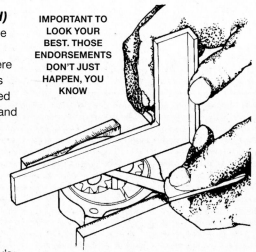

IMPORTANT TO LOOK YOUR BEST. THOSE ENDORSEMENTS DON'T JUST HAPPEN, YOU KNOW

FIG 13•20 **BEARD SQUARE FOR BACKS TO TRIM THEIR STUBBLE JUST SO**

7. Richie McCaw (New Zealand)

World record cap holder, with 148 Tests. Played the offside line better than anyone before or since, leading to rumours that the midwives couldn't find him in the maternity ward as he was born offside. Captained New Zealand to two consecutive World Cups, the first of which he played with a broken foot.

8. Sergio Parisse (Italy)

Superman in a non-super side: Italy's one indisputable world-class player of modern times. If he'd played for another country, or if he'd been an Italian footballer, he'd have been world famous. Plays his club rugby for Stade Francais.

Model history

1823

William Webb Ellis, a pupil at Rugby School, 'with a fine disregard for the rules of football as played in his time first took the ball in his arms and ran with it.' There's always one like that in any school football team, and they're always, to use the technical term, a bit of a git.

1871

The Rugby Football Union (RFU) is founded. 21 clubs and schools attend the meeting and become founder members, but Wasps aren't among them: they turn up at the wrong pub, on the wrong day, at the wrong time. This is, of course, the most rugby thing ever.

1871

Scotland beat England in the first ever international match. Scottish supporters agree to a period of time beyond which they will no longer gloat about this victory. That period still has 52 years left to run.

BOOT POLISH AND DUBBIN, MY BOY. THAT'S HOW TO CARE FOR YOUR BOOTS

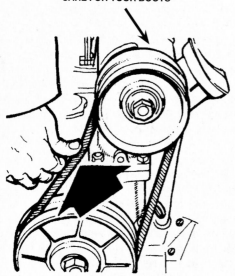

FIG 13•21 **RUGBY FOOTWEAR: CARE AND MAINTENANCE**

'History' in rugby terms can also involve the sort of blood feud beloved of warring Balkan clans, where the response to the question 'how did this all start?' involves bringing out maps from 1878 and historical records from a century even before that.

1886

Russian police clamp down on rugby matches being played in the country because they consider it 'brutal and liable to incite demonstrations and riots.' Quite right too. Being brutal and inciting riots is the job of the Russian police themselves.

1886

Ireland, Scotland and Wales form the first international rugby board. England refuse to join, and then wonder why everyone hates them.

1895

Twenty clubs from Yorkshire, Lancashire and Cheshire resign from the RFU and set up what becomes rugby league. Their beef with the RFU is twofold: the northern clubs want to pay their players, and they think the RFU is full of 'soft southern jessies'.

1931

France is suspended from international rugby amid suspicions that the rules on paying players are being broken. The French? Breaking rules? Offering backhanders? Zut alors!

1940

The Nazi-collaborating Vichy regime in France works hard to re-establish amateur rugby on the grounds that 'its ethos appeals to the German view of the purity of sport.'

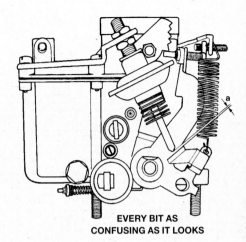

**EVERY BIT AS
CONFUSING AS IT LOOKS**

FIG 13·22 **THE MACHINATIONS OF
INTERNATIONAL RUGBY POLITICS**

1995

Rugby becomes professional following a long period of 'shamateurism'. England captain Will Carling is sacked after referring to the RFU committee as '57 old farts'. The accuracy of his statement is questioned, though only on the grounds that he may have got the exact number wrong.

2000

Italy joins the Six Nations. Italy arrives for the first match with its sunglasses on its forehead, driving a Ferrari, exclaiming 'ciao! Bella!' at every passing woman, and gesticulating wildly with its fork between mouthfuls of pasta with broccoli.

Glossary

Phrase	Meaning
110%	Standard unit of effort given by the boys
36	Nickname of Billy Twelvetrees, from the way his Irish club captain Geordan Murphy pronounces his name
Against the run of play	Somehow they've fluked a try
BIL	The name given to the cuddly toy lion that the youngest member of the Lions squad must take everywhere with him. Stands for British and Irish Lions
Bill	What the Aussies call the Webb Ellis Trophy awarded to the world champions. Short for William (Webb Ellis)
Busier than a one-armed bricklayer in Baghdad	Required to contribute to a strenuous defensive effort
Chiropractor	Nickname of Samoa's Brian Lima, whose tackles were so ferocious that they were thought to rearrange the bones of the recipient
Crash ball	A large man taking a pass at pace and running straight at the opposition. Not subtle. Not pretty. Effective
Dug deep	What the boys had to do to hang on for the win
Dummy	To pretend to pass the ball but actually keep hold of it in an attempt to fool the defender. What that defender feels like if he falls for it
Garryowen	A high short punt behind the defending team. Also known as an 'up-and-under'. Pertinent if your name is either Gary Owen or Uppan Under
Going through the phases	Four unbroken minutes of enormous men running into each other at close range
Going upstairs	Asking the TMO for clarity. Not literally 'going upstairs'
Good tourist	Someone better at drinking than playing
Group of Death	Any tournament pool where the number of decent teams is greater than the number of qualifying places available
Hairs on the back of your neck	Compulsory reference whenever 'Land Of My Fathers' is played at the Principality Stadium in Cardiff.
Hard yards	See 'going through the phases'
Hospital pass	A pass which arrives at the same time as three of the opposition
How's your father, a bit of	A 30-man brawl

Interception	To catch a pass intended for the opposition. To regret said catch when you realise you have to sprint 80 metres to score a try
Knows the way to the tryline	Surely pretty much a prerequisite?
Looking for work	The winger is bored and cold standing out on the touchline and is getting in everyone's way as he tries to stave off frostbite and existential ennui
Lovely little offload	Flash git doing the old back-of-the-hand pass
Mad Dog	Nickname of former England player Lewis Moody, for his total and hilarious disregard of his own safety while playing
Maori sidestep	Bashing straight through the tackler
Mercurial	Inconsistent
Momentum, have the	Won the previous game
Need to do the simple things well	Need to stop showing off
No more than they deserve	A meaningless consolation try with a minute to go
Not that sort of player	Exactly that sort of player
Pill	The ball
Plan B, switching to	We're 42-0 down at half time
Pretty average	Woeful
Radar working	Kicking his goals
Raging Potato	Nickname of follicly challenged Irish hooker Keith Wood
Scotland's year, this could be	Annual proclamation. Annual disappointment
Snow on it, came down with	A ball kicked extremely high. Also meteorologically impossible, even when it is snowing, as the nimbostratus clouds that produce snow start at c.1,500 feet
Thanks for coming	A spectacular tackle
The crowd will tell you if this one goes through	Or you could just watch it yourself
The first 20 minutes will be crucial	As opposed to the second, third and fourth 20 minutes
Wanted it more	The reason one side won

Fault diagnosis

Fault	Diagnosis	Treatment
One of your players is a lunatic	He's a flanker	They're all like that. Sorry.
You can't play rugby like the French	You're not French	Become French. But consider this carefully before taking the plunge.
Referee has made the wrong decision	Referee needs glasses	Referee should go to Specsavers
Opposition player is wearing lurid orange boots	Opposition player is a flash git who needs a good kicking	Give him a good kicking
It feels like you're running through treacle	It's Sunday morning and you have a hangover	Keep sweating it out. You'll be fine after half-time.
Everyone hates the team you support	You support Harlequins	They'll hate you anyway, so you might as well try and beat them
You're in a crowd of people who seem to have Tourette's	You're on the terraces at a football match and the game is not going your team's way	Either leave or accept it'll all be over soon enough anyway
You need the toilet urgently	You have drunk several pints before the game started	Head towards exit 28 now
Sixty million people think they can do your job better than you can	You are England head coach	Blow the Grand Slam. Proceed to next major tournament. Beat first good team you meet. Lose to second good team you meet.
You have control of players who are doing impossibly brilliant things.	You are playing Rugby19 on Playstation	Turn off the TV and return to normal life
You've lost a yard of pace	You never had that yard of pace in the first place	Ponder whether this is satisfactory or unsatisfactory
Your rugby shirt is tighter than it was last season	It must have shrunk in the wash	Resolve not to wash it again. Not that it'll make any difference, as well you know in your heart of hearts.
All the home nations have gone out of the World Cup	The southern hemisphere teams are just better. Sorry.	No treatment available. Just accept it as part of the yawning futility of being a rugby fan.
There's no rugby on TV	It's the off season. For God's sake, don't the players deserve a rest?	Condescend to watch football

Conclusion

A small story to show what a great game rugby is, in every way.

Abdelatif Benazzi started out playing rugby in his Moroccan hometown of Oujda, travelling to matches on the wooden seats of fourth-class train carriages. He ended up winning 79 caps for France, and along the way became the first North African Muslim to captain the country.

But Benazzi was always more than just what the French call a 'rugbyman'. The racial abuse he suffered early in his career, not just from fans but from opponents and even teammates, instilled in him a keen sense of injustice. He now sits on the Immigration Committee, an apolitical body aimed at helping immigrants integrate into French society. He visits prisons and tells inmates that there is a better way for them: a message which carries some weight when delivered by a 2m-tall man mountain who never knowingly took a backward step himself.

He has spoken eloquently of how rugby has taught him much about life, about balancing the demands of the collective with the personal space of the individual. There is, he maintains, no conflict between the freedom to practise his religion and the need to accept and obey the laws of a secular society.

But if you really want to know Benazzi's character, here it is. In the 1995 World Cup semi-final, France played the hosts South Africa on a sodden Durban pitch. Right at the end of the match, with France trailing 19-15, Benazzi launched himself at the line. A try would win France the match. He was held up by a couple of Springboks. Players on both sides dived into the melee, to push their man forward or to resist. Referee Derek Bevan peered into the sea of bodies and whistled: no try. Benazzi, he said, had not grounded the ball over the line.

To this day Benazzi, a man as honest as the day is long, maintains that the try was good. But he knows too that the referee's word is law: no ifs, no buts, no argument. France were out; South Africa were through to the final.

That final, of course, was when Nelson Mandela walked out onto the pitch at Ellis Park wearing the Springbok jersey, for so long the tunic of the oppressor: when thousands of Afrikaners in the stadium, seeing this, rose as one and chanted 'Nelson! Nelson!' Morné du Plessis, the Springbok manager, described it as 'a moment of magic, a moment of wonder. It was fairytale stuff. It was Sir Galahad: 'My strength is as the strength of ten, because my heart is pure.'

Benazzi was one of the spectators in Ellis Park that day. Some years later, he ran into du Plessis at a rugby function, and inevitably the chat turned to the games in question. 'We cried like hell when we lost to you guys,' Benazzi said. 'But when I went to the final I cried again, because I realised it was more important for us not to be there, that something was happening before my eyes that was more important than victory or defeat in a game of rugby.'

Titles in the Haynes Explains series

Now that Haynes has explained Rugby, you can progress
to our full size manuals on car maintenance (more wings,
props and hooks), *Viking Warrior Manual* (for a few handy
tips), *Combat Medicine Manual* (when the injuries get
serious) and the *Beer Manual* (to celebrate your team's win).

There are Haynes manuals on just about everything
– but let us know if we've missed one.

Haynes.com